Contemporary Costa Rican Poetry

Contemporary Costa Rican Poetry

A Bilingual Anthology

Selected by
Carlos Francisco Monge
Translated by
Victor S. Drescher

Edited by
ESCUELA DE LITERATURA Y CIENCIAS DEL LENGUAJE
Co-sponsored by

Indiana University of Pennsylvania

UNA
UNIVERSIDAD
NACIONAL
COSTA RICA

CR861.08
C761c

> Contemporary Costa Rican Poetry: A Bilingual
> Anthology / Selected by Carlos Francisco
> Monge; translated by Victor S. Drescher.
> — 1 ed. — Heredia, C.R.: Universidad
> Nacional. Escuela de Literatura y Ciencias
> del Lenguaje, 2012.
> 155 p.; 28 cm.
> ISBN 978-9968-9863-4-2
> 1. POESÍA COSTARRICENSE 2. LITERA-
> TURA COSTARRICENSE 3. LITERATURA
> CONTEMPORÁNEA I. Monge, Carlos Francisco,
> 1951- II. Drescher, Victor S.

Indiana University of Pennsylvania

UNA
UNIVERSIDAD
NACIONAL
COSTA RICA

CONTENTS

PREFACE

Contemporary Costa Rican poetry flows from the same watershed as the other main currents of modern day Spanish American poetry. At the same time, it has blazed its own trails and found ways to express its own unique reality, history, and circumstances as a Central American country.

For a relatively small country about the size of West Virginia, Costa Rica has a well-developed poetic tradition and produces a considerable amount of poetry. And yet it is surprising how little attention it has gotten internationally. There are, of course, a few authors whose work has been recognized in other countries, in academic circles and among literary critics. And there have been serious overviews of the work, consisting of essays, anthologies, and university theses. But, in general terms, recognition of Costa Rican poetry outside Costa Rica has been slight.

The development of this genre in Costa Rica began with the Spanish American *Modernismo* (1900-1920), and was clearly influenced by French Symbolism and Aestheticism. The "new world" poetry, called *mundonovismo* (1920-1930), followed and was more closely tied to the themes, life, and conditions in American nature. Later came the avant-gard movements that transformed experimental styles and practices to such an extent, especially during the decade of the 1930's. Toward the middle of the twentieth century, Costa Rican poetry made its move toward modernity: new currents, new esthetic choices, new perceptions of history and of the country itself, brought about a notable reorientation and renovation of the poetry that was being written. Next came a period dominated by what was known as social poetry (1960-1980). This poetry focused on the political situation and on pointing out, from an aesthetic perspective and with a strong bias toward its victims, the topics of injustice, repression, and neglect, topics so evident in the sociopolitical reality of Central America.

Nowadays, Costa Rican poetry has not abandoned those themes in any way, but has turned toward other horizons that are less local but equally important. Contemporary Costa Rican poets perceive reality from a much broader and much more complicated set of circumstances. The world can no longer be reduced to a village, a country, or even a region. Costa Rica has been globalized, whether we like it or not. We are part, possibly a small part, but a part just the same, of a history that is being written by powerful forces: politics, technology, ideology, the military, commerce, bioethics, and communications. The contemporary world, the world of the first decade of the twenty-first century, is a very different place compared to what it was fifty years ago. The ways we represent reality have changed, and so has poetry.

The poems selected for this anthology have all been written and published since 1990. The variety of themes and use of language in each and every case is a representative sample (although somewhat small for the moment), of the poetry that is currently being written in Costa Rica. As you will see by the date of birth of the authors, we have included at least four generations: the generation that was tied to the avant-gard movement, the one that was swept up in the modernity of the middle of the last century, the one that wrote social poetry and finally the generation that is interpreting the complexity of present history.

We are offering here a collection of poetry, along with original translations by Victor S. Drescher, for the English-speaking reader who, up until now, has only heard of the occasional Costa Rican poet or the odd poem found in an anthology, but who has never had an overview of Costa Rican poetry.

Carlos Francisco MONGE

TRANSLATOR'S FOREWORD

Borrowing the title of one of the jewels of nineteenth-century French poetry, I would like to invite you to take a trip with me through the world of contemporary Costa Rican poetry. Whereas Baudelaire was beckoning his reader to enter a static tableau of the "Old World" of the 1800's, where everything was "luxury and calm," we, on the other hand, are about to enter the dynamic new world of late twentieth and early twenty-first century Costa Rica where, in the words of Carlos Cortés, the quetzal is "jade fletched with terrifying branches" and a "fiery hummingbird shimmers, his head on fire and mouth flaming." The setting that Baudelaire depicts is one dominated by "order and beauty." Carlos Rafael Duverrán, however, lives in a modern city which he calls his "labyrinth" and, in spite of its disdain for art and love for glitter, it is his lot and he loves it like it is. So much for *"luxe, calme et volupté."*

It is my sincere hope that you will enjoy this voyage as much as I did, and I want to take this opportunity to thank my longtime friend and esteemed colleague, Carlos Francisco Monge, one of the poets included in this anthology, for proposing that we do this in the first place, and for his tireless support. Without his seemingly limitless energy, as well as the unequalled proofreading skills of Sherry Gapper, this project would have never come to fruition.

Victor S. Drescher
March 22, 2012

ACKNOWLEDGEMENTS

The anthologist and the translator wish to thank all those people and institutions that have made this book possible. Above all, we are grateful to the authors or their successors who authorized us to include their poems; and to the School of Languages and Literature of the Universidad Nacional, Costa Rica (UNA), for having accepted to publish it, as well as to the Indiana University of Pennsylvania (IUP), as a co-sponsor. In addition, we again express our appreciation for Sherry Gapper's editing and advice on the translation, and for Ricardo Monge's technical assistance with the layout, overall design and cover artwork.

ISAAC FELIPE AZOFEIFA

ALEGRÍA

Mi patria es este pequeñísimo lugar
perdido entre todos los lugares.
Mínimo y pobre lugar de mis pasos.

De pronto lo he visto cuando andaba
adentro de mí mismo
que es como volverse adentro de la mirada,
como volverse ciego,
como romperse el corazón
y echarse a andar por sus venas.

Entro en mi sangre, sí, pero salgo al paisaje,
al recuerdo,
al aire calmo de la aldea, al pueblo insistente,
mi pueblo,
al cielo de todos. ¡Oh alegría!

ISAAC FELIPE AZOFEIFA

HAPPINESS

My homeland is this tiny little place
lost among all the other places.
A humble little place where I walk.

I saw it suddenly as I was strolling
inside myself
which is like turning your look inward,
like going blind,
like breaking into your heart
and taking off walking in your veins.

I go into my bloodstream, true, but I step out
                              [into the landscape,
into the memories,
into the calm surroundings of the village, its persistent
                              [people,
my town,
and everyone's sky. What happiness!

EL YIGÜIRRO DE LA MADRUGADA

Sonoro, el yigüirro irrita la madrugada.
Es necio. Reiterativo. Hace silencios bruscos.
Conversa. Pregunta. Espera. Repite.
El día se niega a amanecer.
La noche prolonga lo oscuro
y el yigüirro dale que dale
con su canto y sus pausas.
Sus atropellos.

De pronto, la hembra lo llama.
Pájaro en celo el yigüirro calla.
Tan largo calla que me duermo
hasta que de bruces,
sonoro el día se echa sobre el mundo
con silencios,
conversaciones, ruidos, repitiéndose
sin fin y alejándose
agarrado a mi mano
como si ambos trajéramos en el pecho
con canto y todo,
al yigüirro de la madrugada.

THE EARLY MORNING ROBIN*

Loud, the robin agitates the early morning.
He's obnoxious. He's repetitive. Then abruptly silent.
He chats. He questions. He pauses. He reiterates.
Day refuses to break.
Night prolongs the darkness
and the robin keeps it up
with his song and his silences.
His outrage.

Out of nowhere the female calls him.
Always in heat, the robin hushes.
He is quiet so long that I fall back asleep
until suddenly,
noisily, day erupts upon the world
with its silences,
with its conversations, its outbursts, repeating itself
endlessly, and going away
holding my hand
as if both of us were carrying within our breast,
chirping and all,
the early morning robin.

EL SUEÑO INFINITO

La poesía es el poema

El ojo del puente contempla su agua
y piensa.
Y el agua pasa y bebe el pensamiento
y el pensamiento se va navegando y golpeándose
entre piedras, malezas, tormentas y remansos
hasta el mar sin límites, la mar infinita.

Pétreo el puente viejo de siglos
decorado de algas y líquenes,
viento y lluvia le cantan sus antiguas
melodías. Lo visten lianas y parásitas.
Un roble joven se recuesta en su espalda.
Un día crujió la tierra. Era un dios
el puente, sosteniendo el mundo.

Abrazado a su río el ojo insomne
del puente, piensa y sueña.
Y el viento viene y alza el sueño
y se lo lleva por los surcos del cielo
y arroja sus semillas lo más lejos de lo lejos
y el sueño se vuelve alimento de los pájaros
y su flor alegra el sol.

Todo está ahí, el reto de la piedra,
su mirada fija como una pregunta
esperando respuesta;

THE ENDLESS DREAM

The poetry is in the poem

The eye of the bridge ponders its water
and thinks.
And the water passes and drinks in the thought
and the thought slides along striking
stones, weeds, storms, and backwaters
before it reaches the endless sea, the infinite sea.

The old stone bridge, centuries old
covered with algae and lichens,
the wind and rain serenade it
with their ancient melodies. It is clothed in vines
                                                 [and parasites.
A young oak tree reclines on its back.
In days gone by it made the earth tremble. It was a god
this bridge, holding up the Earth.

Clinging to its river, the sleepless eye
of the bridge thinks and dreams.
And the wind comes and lifts the dream
and carries it off through the furrows of the sky
and scatters its seeds farther than far
and the dream becomes food for the birds
and its blossoms brighten the sun.

It's all there, the defiant stone,
its frozen stare like a question
waiting for an answer;

el ojo sin párpado del puente
eternamente pensándose, soñándose,
Buscándose a sí mismo entre el mar sin memoria
y el cielo sin límites, insondable.
¡Oh forma que no cesa de crearse,
oh desolada lágrima del que sueña!

the lidless eye of the bridge
eternally thinking, dreaming,
searching for itself between the timeless sea
and the limitless sky, unfathomable.
Oh form of unceasing re-creation,
oh tormented tear of he who dreams!

JORGE CHARPENTIER

AMANTE CON AMOR CONDENA

Mi amor recluido.
Pobre amor sin nada que le abrigue
en las noches de frío.

Miserable amor.
Tiene que pagar a cambio de un espejo
y muere asesinado cada noche por la culpa.
Aguarda los domingos,
entre esperanzar y dolerse,
que algún pariente madre
visite con noticias su prisión.

Mi pobre amor recluido.
Le miente a su tristeza.
Inventa viajes libre.
Cada día del día ensancha las paredes
y quiere amordazar la piel del vidrio:
locura de engañarse y opacar.

Mi entrañable y veraz amor recluido
que cumple sin condena la condena.

Cuánto habré de esperar para verte salir,
Alegre, amor, alegre
y para siempre siempre perdonado.

JORGE CHARPENTIER

LOVER CONDEMNS WITH LOVE

My reclusive love.
Poor love with nothing to warm you
on cold nights.

Wretched love.
Forced to pay for a mirror
and dying every night at the hand of guilt.
You await Sundays
torn between getting up hope and feeling the pain
of some concerned relative
dropping by your cell with news.

My poor reclusive love.
You tell lies to your sadness.
You make up carefree travels.
Each day by day you widen the walls
and try to muzzle the window's beam:
the madness of fooling yourself and making it darker.

My most affectionate and true wretched love
serving the sentence without being condemned.

How long will I have to wait to see you free,
happy, love, happy,
and always and forever forgiven.

ENTRE MADRUGAR Y ENTRAR LA NOCHE

entre madrugar y entrar la noche
me topo obreras y obreros
mojados de arroz
y quién sabe qué agua.

caminan con premura y señorío,
y para qué.
no sonríen.

a las cinco de la tarde
los veo con regreso
sin haber alcanzado
el pan de la mañana.

me duele
su aguardiente apresurado,
su mano callosa
como gaviota en llamas
suplicando
para que no los dejen
solitarios y solos
perdidos con hambre
en el centro del mundo.

comen con los dedos.
acarician botón a botón
programa de dormirse
bajo alero surtidor empobrecido.

FROM MORNING TILL NIGHT

from morning till night
I run into laborers
running on juice
from who knows where.

they walk quickly and proudly,
and who knows why?
they don't smile.

at five in the afternoon
I see them return
without having earned
bread for the morrow.

I can feel
their hurried liquor,
their calloused hands
like sea gulls in flame
begging
not to be left
abandoned and alone
lost and hungry
in the center of everything.

they eat hurriedly.
they lovingly caress button after button
a program to fall asleep by
beneath bewildering and impoverished eaves.

recuerdan que mañana.
recuerdan.
nunca miran hacia atrás.
reduerdan que mañana
otra vez tendrán que aparentar
a las cinco en punto de la tarde.

they remember that tomorrow.
they remember.
they never look back.
they remember that tomorrow
they will once again have to put on a show
at exactly five in the afternoon.

CON EL BASTÓN Y LAS MANOS

con el bastón y las manos
qué guapa está la madre.
qué guapa está
con sus huesos curvos
haciendo catedrales
y paseando en su regazo
delantal de recuerdos.

cuando se amorosa
alrededor
de su seco río
y hace que crezca un lirio
donde nadie esperaba
que creciera,
qué guapa está.

qué guapa está la madre
con sus ojeras,
luces para que la sigan
sin perderse.

guapa está y en despedida,
acurrucándose en su vientre
y cantando cuna de canción
a los hijos que tuvo
y que no tuvo.

WITH HER CANE AND HER HANDS

with her cane and her hands
see how beautiful mother is.
how beautiful she is
with her curved bones
imitating cathedrals
and showing off an apron of memories
on her lap.

when her love outpours
over her dried up riverbed
and makes a lily grow
where no one expected
that a lily would ever grow,
how beautiful she is.

how beautiful mother looks
with the bags under her eyes,
lights so they can follow her
without getting lost.

beautiful she is and saying farewell,
curled up in a ball
a singing cradle of songs
to the children she had
and those that she didn't.

CARLOS RAFAEL DUVERRÁN

ESTE ES MI LABERINTO

Mi laberinto es éste, mi ciudad y mi vida.
Y no sé aún si el arte, si los sueños perdidos o recobrados
en la mayor vigilia podrán aquí salvarse,
echar raíces o garras para sobrevivir.
Este es mi laberinto. Llega la noche y otra noche
y otro día y otro día, y nada cambia. Las mismas calles,
las mismas estatuas asombradas de haber nacido
a formas. No sé si nos salvaremos,
no sé si mi generación encontrará su artista,
el que grabe su tiempo y su verdad para siempre,
no sé si sobrevivirán los cantos o la mala prosa
                                        [de los políticos.
Este es mi laberinto, en él me tocó y así lo amo,
a pesar de su desamor por el arte y la verdad acuñada,
de su pasión por el oropel, por la falsa esmeralda
y el ámbar corrompido. Lugar de oídos sordos
y rostros fantasmales (¿adónde irán las palabras
sopladas justamente?). Este es mi laberinto.

CARLOS RAFAEL DUVERRÁN

THIS IS MY LABYRINTH

This is my labyrinth, my city and my life.
And I still don't know if art, if dreams lost,
or those recovered during long sleepless nights,
                              [can be saved here,
can grow roots, or maybe talons, in order to survive.
This is my labyrinth. Night becomes day,
day becomes night, and nothing changes. The same streets,
the same statues that seem surprised to have been born
and taken shape. I do not know if we can save ourselves,
I do not know if my generation will find its artist,
the one that will record its time and its truth once
                              [and for all,
nor do I know if the music or the poor prose of politicians
                              [will survive.
This is my labyrinth, it is my lot and I love it like it is,
little matter its disdain for art, its fabricated truth,
its love for glitter, for fake emeralds
and tainted amber. A place of deaf ears
and phantasmagoric faces (just what becomes of
whispered truths?) This is my labyrinth.

RETRATO DE NIÑA

Nunca se sabe qué pasó. Pasan como nubes,
como olas o sirenas y uno se pregunta qué fue
                                    [de aquella gracia
que apenas empezaba a descifrar. La impresión
                                    [de algo intenso,
las ráfagas de un vértigo es todo lo que queda
de un gran fulgor. Y el retrato interior, que se transforma
y se va desgastando de tanto andar con uno
                                    [por ciudades y pueblos.
Y tú la has dibujado en figura de niña: su rostro
                                    [en el grabado
más tierno aún y verdadero. En lugar de crecer
dentro de ti se ha ido regresando
hasta ser lo esencial, esa pequeña niña
(en la textura del papel se inscribe la ligereza y el asombro)
ese deseo de ser
            esa suave insolencia
de no ser todavía una respuesta.

PORTRAIT OF A LITTLE GIRL

One never knows what happened. They pass by like clouds,
like waves or mermaids and one wonders where did it go
that grace that was just starting to figure things out.
                    [The impression of something intense,
gusts of vertigo are all that remain
of a brilliant flash. And your mind carries a picture,
                              [which is changing
and wearing out from so much walking together through
                              [cities and towns.
And you have drawn her as a little girl: her features
                              [in the sketch
even more tender and real. Instead of growing
inside of you, she has been slipping away
toward that essential being, that little girl
(her lightness and her wonderment are felt in the texture
                              [of the paper)
that desire to be
            that soft insolence
remains a mystery.

EN MEDIO DE LAS COSAS

En medio de las cosas
        del trajín nácar de los días
oímos el agudo sonido
        que llegaba de nuevo
sin pensar que pudiera traer para nosotros
un latido de antigua madera.

Vimos la edición nueva del verde
y repasamos con calma las hojas encendidas
aún vivas, de la estación;
de pronto
una luz entra y se fija
        en medio de la casa,
como la espada de un ángel que llegara en la noche
puesta ahí queda ardiendo
        llameando,
entonces comprendimos,
apartamos las hojas amarillas, el cobre derrotado,
lavamos el aire crepuscular, el manifiesto
              [primero de la escarcha,
trajimos ramas para hacer un dulce fuego.
Y no volvimos a sentirnos solos.

IN THE MIDST OF EVERYTHING

In the midst of the gilded hustle and bustle
                              of everyday life
we heard the piercing sound
                    all over again
without realizing that it could bring us
a new heartbeat from ancient timbers.

We saw the new round of greenery
and calmly revisited the season's brilliant leaves
all still so alive;
suddenly a light comes in and settles
                              in the midst of the house,
like the sword of an angel that comes in the night
it stood there burning,
                    flaming.
It was then that we understood,
we put away the yellowing pages, the corroding copper,
we cleared out the dawn air,
                          the first signs of frost,
we brought in branches to make a small fire.
And we never felt lonely again.

© Carlos Kidd

MAYRA JIMÉNEZ

CARTA

Sí,
de esto hace muchos años.
Tu cuerpo era un tanto más delgado
y usabas jeans.
Estuvimos en reuniones académicas
hablando sobre el método,
en reuniones políticas,
uno frente al otro
(por la noche, cada quien con su pareja).
Nos cruzábamos
por los pasillos de la Facultad.
intercambiábamos palabras,
serios.

Con él soñé
pero oculté los sueños:
   —me poseyó de pie
   en la oficina,
   sobre el escritorio,
   entre los libros de la biblioteca.

Ah, sueños vergonzosos.

Ahora,
en el momento en que te escribo

MAYRA JIMÉNEZ

EMAIL

Yes,
That was a long time ago.
You were a little thinner
and you wore jeans.
We were in academic meetings
talking about methodology,
in political meetings,
facing each other
(at night, each with his or her partner).
We crossed paths
in the hallways at the university.
We exchanged words,
we were serious.

I dreamt of him
but I hid my dreams:
        —he took me standing
        in the office,
        on the desk,
        among the books in the library.

Ah, shameful dreams.

Now, as I write to you
I begin sending viruses over the internet

empiezo a mandar virus por internet
a Greenwich
para cambiar las fechas
y tenerte "accanto mio", "tremante"
pronto, sin esperar al miércoles.

Me asusta que esto sea un espejismo sin desierto
y despertar en no sé qué paraje de la nada.

Pero no, estás aquí
con tu oler tan propio,
con tu anhelar tan lejos
y tu venir tan cerca,
con tu pasión tan clara,
con tu mirar oscuro,
tus muslos fuertes
y tu bailar descalzo.
Estás aquí con el amor secreto.

to Greenwich
to change the dates
and have you "accanto mio," "tremante"
soon, without waiting till Wednesday.

It frightens me that this could be a mirage without a desert
and I could awake in who knows what nothing of a place.

But no, you are here
with your unique smell,
with your longing so far away
and your coming so nearby,
with your passion so bright,
and your gaze so dark
your strong thighs
and your barefoot dancing.
You are here with our secret love.

REENCUENTRO

En este pueblo donde habito
llueve casi todo el año. La mañana gris,
la tarde.
Noches oscuras.
En el corto tiempo del verano
el aire es cálido, el cielo azul
(en mágica transformación).

Conduciendo el auto
llegué de noche a tu encuentro.
En mi memoria
puedo reconstruir
poco a poco
tus palabras
el color de tus ojos avellana
y lo que mi cuerpo rozando a tu cuerpo le decía.
En mi memoria tengo
el modo como giras
al ritmo de la música
con tu oído agudísimo, finísimo,
cuando escuchas a Dvorák
en esta sala chica,
aquí,
en el verano breve
sobre este pueblo neblinoso.

Ven, entonces,
desde tu pequeño estudio

WE MEET AGAIN

In this town where I live
it rains nearly all year. Gray mornings,
and afternoons.
Dark nights.
In the brief summertime
the air is warm, the sky blue
(a magical transformation).

Driving the car
I got to meet you at night.
In my memory
I can reconstruct
your words
step by step,
the color of your hazelnut eyes
and what my body brushing against your body was saying.
I still remember
the way you moved
to the rhythm of the music
with your sharp ear, so fine,
when listening to Dvorak
in this small room,
here,
in the short summer
above this misty town.

Come, then,
from your small study

(iluminado por un pájaro a colores,
labrado en madera y con mi nombre)
a esta estancia más secreta,
interior, perenne
y juntos nos iremos
en un viaje
que nos conducirá despacio
a destino cierto,
con precisión, exacto,
como un astro
desplazándose cauto entre planetas,
aerolitos y constelaciones.

Ven, amor,
a esta estancia mía
interior, perenne,
llenos de luz mis libros.

(brightened by a colorful wooden bird
with my name on it)
to this secret space of mine
internal, perennial
and we'll go together
on a trip
that will take us slowly
straight to our destination
precisely, exactly,
like a star
moving cautiously through planets,
meteors and constellations.

Come, love,
to this space of mine
internal, perennial
my books are full of light.

EN EL RÍO TAMARINDO

Veo su cuerpo desnudo.
Desatendido se baña mientras yo
lo observo desde la orilla.
(Recuerdo en cuántas camas nos hemos acostado
en cuántas playas,
en cuántas,
siempre temerosos de ser sorprendidos
en la inolvidable noche de pasión).
Ágil
saltas de piedra en piedra,
te pones el pantalón rápido y
seguimos por la colina-montaña
tú con tu mochila verde-olivo
yo con un libro de Nazim Hikmet en mi bolso.

IN THE TAMARINDO RIVER

I see his naked body.
He is swimming by himself
while I watch him from the shore.
(I remember how many beds we have slept in,
on how many beaches
on how many,
always in fear of being surprised
in unforgettable nights of passion).
Graceful,
you jump from stone to stone,
quickly put on your pants
and we go on up the steep hillside
you with your olive green backpack
me with a book by Nazim Himket* in my bag.

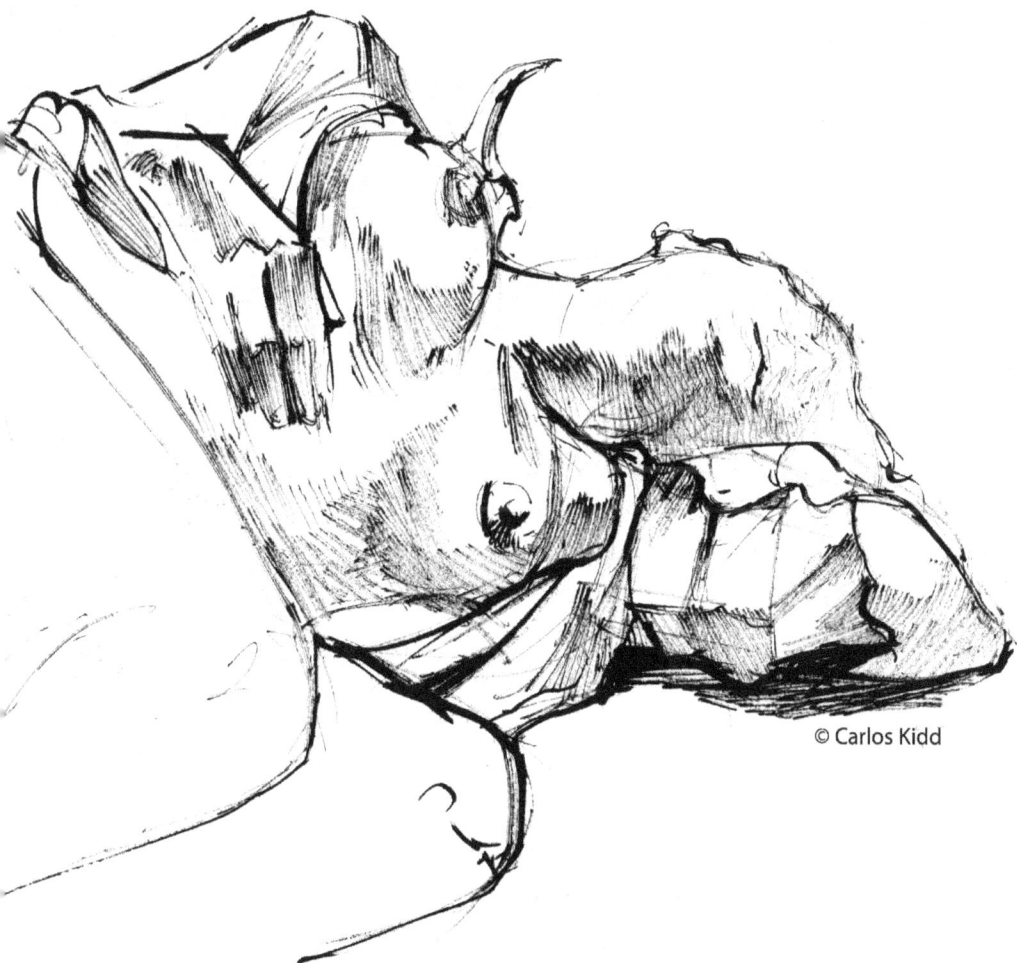

© Carlos Kidd

JULIETA DOBLES

CASA EN EL SUEÑO

Repleta de ventanas antiguas y de hiedras,
dos pisos de silencios y de músicas,
en el paraje límite de mis prados de infancia,
la casa de mis sueños morosos, recurrentes,
se aferra al borde de la niebla
al vacío donde intuyo los ecos y las voces,
los vórtices y abismos, las rocas imprevistas
sobre el lomo del miedo.
Allá afuera, se quedan acechantes,
como el Mar Tenebroso
de los antiguos héroes del olvido.

Detrás de nuestros pasos cerramos con estruendo
su gran puerta de roble, tan firme como un bosque.
Sus muros se acomodan a nuestras decisiones,
abrazos sucesivos que nos aman
detrás de las ventanas y el deseo.
Los paisajes se otean, iluminados
por una extraña luz atardecida
tras los fuertes cristales centenarios.

De pronto nos florecen sorprendidos rosales,
y aquellas buganvilias vibrantes del pasado,
y los geranios que suben, despertándose:
las trepadoras álgidas que en la noche del mundo
han trepado a mi vida, rotundas, auspiciosas.

JULIETA DOBLES

THE HOUSE IN MY DREAM

Covered with old windows and ivy,
two stories of silence and music
at the outer edge of my childhood meadows,
the home of my slow recurrent dreams
clings to the edge of the fog
in a void where I sense echoes and voices,
whirlwinds and abysses, treacherous rocks
on the back of fear.
They lie out there in waiting,
like the Dark Sea
of heroes of antiquity long forgotten.

Behind us we close with a thud
its great oaken door, as solid as a forest.
Its walls adjust to our decisions,
successive embraces that love us
behind the windows and the desire.
Landscapes look over each other, lit
by a strange afternoon glow
through the solid century-old window panes.

Suddenly surprised rose bushes blossom for us,
and those brilliant bougainvillea from the past,
and geraniums climbing, awakening
the determined climbers that climbed into my life,
auspicious, resounding, while the world slept.

Invaden nuestro techo alegremente,
llenan tejas y muros de púrpuras y aroma,
hasta que por su peso se desprenden y caen,
cubriendo mis almohadas de risas infantiles.

Sólo una casa es —y quizás todas—
al borde de los sueños.

They happily invade our roof
filling the tiles and walls with shades of purple and aromas,
until their own weight detaches them and they fall,
covering my pillows with childish laughter.

It's just a house—or maybe all houses—
on the edge of a dream.

DESCUBRIMIENTO

Vivo en la posibilidad
EMILY DISCKINSON

Yo voy viviendo
de los retazos
que el azar dispone,
del tiempo que me das,
insuficiente siempre,
pero eterno en sí mismo
y raro paraíso.

Por eso cuando llegas,
un fervor de ansiedades me recorre,
se llena mi garganta de cielos encrespados,
subo hasta la sonrisa carnosa de tu boca
y beso y muerdo y me apresuro,
como si en esos minutos demenciales
se me fuera la vida
y su puntual de gozo.
Vivir es eso: retomar día a día
los amores, las fiebres, las estrellas
que sorprenden por dentro nuestros años.
Por eso cada encuentro que tramamos
es un punto de gloria que agradezco.

Y tu cuerpo, sinfonía del tacto
frente a mi soledad,
sobrecogida de ansias.

DISCOVERY

I dwell in the realm of possibility
EMILY DICKINSON

I get by living
on the scraps
that fate provides,
the time that you give me,
never enough,
yet eternal in its miniature
and unequaled paradise.

That's why when you arrive
intense anxiety ripples through me,
filling my throat with choppy skies.
I rise to the fleshy smile of your mouth
and kiss and bite and hurry,
as if in those few insane minutes
life may escape me,
taking with it my support beam of pleasure.
This is life: picking back up day after day
the love, the fever, the stars
that surprise us in our years.
That's why every encounter that we pull off
is a glorious event for which I am thankful.

And your body, a symphony of touching,
confronts my loneliness,
overwhelmed by anxiety.

Tu mano, entonces,
va construyendo mi hermosura.
Ella recorre, ansiosa, cada rincón,
cada pliegue, cada desaliento,
con el matiz certero del deseo.

Así somos, amigo,
salvos y bellos como nunca,
en medio de esa música
que urdimos cuerpo a cuerpo,
como un escalofrío interminable.

Then your hand
sets about reconstructing my beauty.
It runs nervously over every spot,
each crease, each fold, each depression,
with firm tones of desire.

That's how we are, my friend,
secure and beautiful as never before,
in the midst of that music
that our bodies weave tirelessly
like an unending shiver.

LA CASA ENAMORADA

Mi casa huele a ti.

Se despereza como animal antiguo
y toma tu lento respirar
después de las batallas del amor.
Te vas, pero te quedas
en su atmósfera de bosque anochecido,
cuando el tango final se ha ido tragando
nuestros últimos bríos
y una música mayor,
la del postrer orgasmo,
nos desmaya en las sábanas.

Tú preparas el adiós,
aunque todo tu cuerpo
quiera quedarse aquí,
sobre la cama,
avivando los mínimos
rescoldos de ternura
que aún nos pertenecen.

Pero la casa sabe que te vas
y su atmósfera toda
se impregna de tu olor, de tus palabras,
para hacerlas durar toda la noche
y someterme así, abrupta y tiernamente,
al vértigo de mi soledad
sobre tu cuerpo ido.

THE HOUSE IS IN LOVE

My house smells like you.

It stretches itself like an aged animal
and absorbs your gentle breathing
after love's struggles.
You leave, but you're still here
in its atmosphere of forest at nightfall,
when the last tango has swallowed up
what energy we had left
and a grander music,
that of the final orgasm,
makes us collapse on the sheets.

You get ready to say goodbye,
although every fiber of your body
wants to stay here,
on the bed,
stirring the faintest
embers of tenderness
that we still possess.

But the house knows that you are leaving
and its entire being
is impregnated with your smell, with your words,
making them last all night
and exposing me, abruptly and tenderly,
to the dizziness of my loneliness
over your absent body.

Cuando cierras la puerta,
y el último beso se agiganta tras ella,
mi casa toma posesión de tu recuerdo
que asalta las cortinas,
bulle en los recios muros
y cruje entre los verbos de la cama,
como si ese animal hermoso y deseante
que me habita y te habita
fuese su apasionado cómplice,
su conviviente,
su íntimo par
enamorado.

When you close the door,
and the last kiss becomes endless behind it,
my house takes possession of your memory
which lays siege to the curtains,
swarms over the sturdy walls
and rustles through conversations
still lingering in the bed cloths,
as if that beautiful and insatiable beast
that lives within me and within you
were its passionate accomplice,
its partner,
its intimate beloved
equal.

RODRIGO QUIRÓS

CONVERSACIONES CON DEBRAVO

Ahora que estás maduro en el surco celeste,
pienso que cambiaría todo lo que de sueños queda en mí
por darte un simple abrazo.
Y contarte que la tierra está roja de semilla
como a ti te gustaba;
y que los niños nacen intactos hacia el cielo
y el sol es siempre puro, recién brindado a todos.
Y a pesar de alambras y metrallas,
los inocentes cuecen panes inacabables
en cada esquina tejida por las lágrimas.

Yo sigo absorto, Jorge, manejando locuras
de verdor absoluto e inevitables nubes,
rozando a Dios en cada movimiento,
derramando astros nuevos en los pasos.
Pero algo ha cambiado:
mira cómo he crecido: daría todos mis sueños
por darte un solo abrazo en honor de los vivos.

RODRIGO QUIRÓS

CONVERSATIONS WITH DEBRAVO*

Now that you have ripened in the celestial furrow,
I think that I would trade every dream left within me
to have my arm around you for just one moment.
And to tell you that the earth is red with seeds
the way you liked it;
and that children are born intact facing heaven
and the sun is always pure, recently offered up to all.
And that in spite of wire fences and shrapnel,
the innocent bake never-ending loaves of bread
on every street corner knit together with tears.

I continue to be overwhelmed, Jorge,
managing fits of totally green madness
and unavoidable clouds,
rubbing up against God at every turn,
pouring new stars into my footsteps.
But something has changed.
See how I've grown: I would give all of my dreams
to embrace you just one time in honor of the living.

EL MALINFORMADO

The news is always bad
ALDOUS HUXLEY

No leo el periódico. Si tuviera el destino
de que una bomba cayera en mi poema,
ya bien me enteraría
que la cosa es conmigo.
Yo soy el gabinete del milagro,
el loco que ama y ama sin hacer estadísticas de fango,
el pecador que espera perdón y pan,
estrellas y silencios,
auscultando las huellas dolorosas de Cristo.
Y es que percibo, con una lucidez (muy egoísta)
que todo acabará hecho escombros sangrantes
para que venga Él a hacerlo todo nuevo.

¿Qué haré para que sepan
que me gusta el progreso?
¿Ponerme un traje de fatiga,
comprar un rifle con mis pobres ahorros,
pintar insultos de noche en las paredes,
y poner veinte veces
la palabra revolución en cinco versos?
Eso me estropearía la digestión y el poema.
No hay noticias. Sólo muerte alineando prosélitos
para desperdiciar la sangre por un nombre,
consigna, o manifestó
con dientes e intenciones de vampiro.

Contemporary Costa Rican Poetry

THE UNINFORMED

The news is always bad
ALDOUS HUXLEY

I don't read the paper. If it so happened
that a bomb fell on my poem,
I think I would know
that it happened to me.
I am the miracle department,
the madman who loves, and loves without keeping
[petty records,
the sinner who expects food and forgiveness,
stars and silence,
while probing Christ's agonizing footprints.
And it is because I can see clearly (very egotistical)
that all will end in bloody ruin
so that He may come again to make it all new.

What shall I do so that people will know
that I am in favor of progress?
Put on fatigues,
buy a rifle with my meager savings,
spend nights scrawling insults on the walls,
and writing the word *revolution* twenty times in five verses?
That would upset my digestion, as well as the poem.
There is no news. Only death lining up converts
to spill blood for a name,
a slogan, or a manifesto
with a vampire's teeth, and intentions.

Sí estamos muertos, señores, afortunadamente.
Todo se ha dicho ya, nada se ha hecho.
Si muerto tomo el lápiz y sigo con mis versos
es porque espero algo mejor del hombre.

Yes we are dead, ladies and gentlemen, fortunately.
Everything has already been said, nothing has been done.
If after I die I take up my pen and continue writing,
it's because I expect better things from mankind.

ESTE SOL, MI SEÑOR...

Al poeta hermano Guillermo Sáenz Patterson

Este sol, mi Señor, que enciende mariposas
y aligera tu verde y tu rocío,
es también el más lúcido testigo
de aquellos que amanecen sin café ni esperanza,
y persiguen la asistencia del aire en torpes movimientos
que no alcanzan el pan,
los que llevan tu rostro pegado al corazón
en un consuelo que corroen las ratas inclementes,
cotidianos soberbios que escupen en tu cruz...

Mas yo conozco un día en que todos cabremos en tus ojos,
y tu luz girará en pómulos rosados,
en aire firme y sonrisas desnudas.
Cada día se hace tarde.
Perdóname si entiendo que hace falta tu prisa.

THIS SUN, MY LORD

to my fellow poet Guillermo Sáenz-Patterson*

This sun, my Lord, that lights up the butterflies
and brightens your greenery and your morning dew,
is also the most powerful witness
of those who awaken with neither sustenance nor hope,
and who seek help clumsily from thin air
finding no bread,
those who wear your image stamped on their heart,
a consolation that the merciless rats gnaw away,
the haughty who daily spit on your cross...

But I know of that day when we'll all be in your sight,
and your light will shine on rosy cheeks,
on solid air and innocent smiles.
Every day it gets later.
Forgive me if I understand that we need you to hurry.

© Carlos Kidd

CARLOS FRANCISCO MONGE

PROFANACIÓN DEL QUIJOTE

Yo me pregunto a veces
por qué amar a ese tonto de capirote,
a ese sujeto soñador, solemne,
tan metido en sus trasgos,
tan zafio, tan huraño.
Me pregunto si toda la belleza
no es más que una vacía cuchillada en el aire,
un claror en la vista fatigada,
una seña olvidable.
Y más triste es aun
tratar de responderles esas mismas preguntas
a esos chicos menudos, firmes en sus deseos,
con miradas atónitas,
allí sentados ante esta cantera de dudas,
frente a este disfraz de lector traicionado,
poco feliz, perdido.
Si pudiera decirles
que las maderas crujen, ya sin culpa ni gracia,
por el tiempo,
que la noche nos deja subrepticias palabras,
que hay un polvo de siglos
gritando enamorado como si no existiesen
la amargura o la aniquilación.
Pero no hay cómo darles explicación a todo:
ellos saben que la única mentira
es inventar la gloria,

CARLOS FRANCISCO MONGE

DESECRATION OF DON QUIXOTE

Sometimes I ask myself
why should we love this fool in a cape,
this somber, dreaming buffoon
so much in his own world,
so uncouth, such a misfit.
I wonder if all of his attraction
is nothing more than empty stabbing at the air,
a bright flash caused by eyestrain,
a forgettable gesture.
And it is more disheartening still
to try to answer these same questions
when asked by youngsters, so rooted in their world.
With surprised looks
they sit there before this reservoir of doubt,
before this betrayed reader in costume,
unhappy and lost.
If I could just tell them
that the structure groans, through no fault nor merit
                                        [of its own,
but because of time,
that darkness leaves us with its surreptitious words,
a residue of centuries
that shout of love as if
bitterness or annihilation did not exist.
But there is no way to explain everything to them:
they know that the greatest lie

y que sus cuerpos bellos,
tan llenos de sentidos y señales
no habrán de sucumbir.
Yo soy el obcecado,
el soñador, el torpe;
el que página a página redobla sus patrañas,
que a sus horas felices les despoja
de sus mejores palabras, de sus gestos
y de sus figuras.
Y todo mi estupor
como un alud se cae, se precipita
con las manchas del tiempo,
velando armas, huyendo
indigno de su amor.
Yo me pregunto a veces
por qué aman a este tonto, a este sujeto huraño
que los quiere de veras, que los sueña.

is to make up glory of whole cloth,
and that their beautiful young bodies,
so fertile in meaning and gesture,
will never succumb.
I am the stubborn one,
the dreamer, the clumsy fool;
the one who, page upon page,
pumps up their tall tales,
in their happiest hours strips away their best lines,
their expressions and their figures of speech.
Then all of my astonishment
like an avalanche comes crashing in,
sweeping away the age spots,
and I am keeping vigil over my armor,
fleeing, unworthy of his love.
I wonder sometimes
why they love this fool, this outcast
who loves them truly, who dreams them to life.

POEMA DEL ENCINO

¿Hay algo que evitar;
algo como el encino, tan solitario a veces,
tan dispuesto al combate, a las carestías?
¿Es evitable, acaso, la indagación del miedo,
la luz crepuscular,
los pájaros cantando más allá del espejo?
¿Evitable el océano, sus marismas,
los ríos subterráneos que van decolorando nuestros pies
sin dejar rastro apenas?
¿Bastaría algún gesto para detener
la sombra en las axilas
y nos roe, nos roe, capaz de besar e inmovilizar a un tiempo?

Y ese hilo que trepa las paredes, escudriña ventanas,
cava, recorre ponzoñoso cuerpos inolvidables
hasta atarlos al tiempo y a sus laberintos,
¿es posible mirarlo divertidos, nosotros los que apenas
                                        [sabemos
que no hay otro lugar, ni presagios ni ruidos?
¿Y qué fluye en las venas
sino un verdor como acabado y persistente,
una marca serena de los ríos
que atravesados una vez nos dan
ansiedad y esplendor, contemplación y fuga,
un claror y un rumoroso aroma?
¿Cómo evitar los sótanos, las barras de los bares;
cómo impedir que el tiempo se abalance

Contemporary Costa Rican Poetry

THE OAK

Is there anything on earth whose existence we can deny?
Can we deny the existence of the oak, so solitary at times,
so ready for combat, for hard times?
Is there any way to deny the existence of fear,
the pale light at dawn,
birds singing beyond the mirror?
Is the ocean to be denied, its marshlands,
the subterranean rivers that discolor our feet
barely leaving a trace?
Is any gesture enough to halt
the darkness in our armpits
and the gnawing on us, the chewing on us, able to kiss
                              [and make time stand still?

And that thread that climbs the walls, scrutinizes
                              [the windows,
digs, threads poison through unforgettable bodies,
before stitching them to time and to its labyrinths,
can we possibly enjoy looking at it, we who barely know
that there is no other place, no omens nor sounds?
And what flows through our veins
but a persistent worn out greenness,
a serene souvenir of the rivers
that, once crossed, give us
both anxiety and delight, contemplation and flight
a flash of light and a murmuring aroma?
How do we deny the cellars, the bars in the bars;
how do we keep time from pouncing on us

como una bestia agazapada,
sin respuesta o reparo?
¿Hay algo más que masticar palabras,
contra las piedras, contra las mañanas,
en favor de los puertos, los supermercados,
por la gracia del mar y sus calificadas estrellas?
Se quedarán, lo sé, los pájaros cantando,
y el pozo de los deseos
y el agua
y el encino
tan solitario a veces de palabras incluso.

like a crouching beast,
with no excuse and no shame?
Is there anything more than stirring up words,
struggling against the stones, against morning,
cheering for the ports, the supermarkets,
for the grace of the sea and its glorious stars?
They will remain, I know, the birds singing,
the wishing well
and the water
and the oak
so solitary at times, even without these words.

INVITACIÓN A DISOLVER LA MATERIA

Difícil es no hallar solemnidad y encanto
en esta noche de mar, ciudad incluida.
Las ceremonias no se acaban nunca:
olas de ayer, espumas de otros días,
fantasmas encallados, ventanas penumbrosas
y avenidas y cuerpos.
Aquí reina la historia: sus miserias, sus juegos;
la música de antaño no lamenta el pasado
y tu cuerpo y mi cuerpo se deslizan
como buscando espejos, como bosques ardiendo,
frente a esta inmensidad que sin palabras canta,
frente a esta pequeñez parlera
de avenidas y gatos y rincones infectos.
Mira este mar: no son palabras vanas;
cuánto sabio sosiego hay en sus danzas,
cuánta verdad contra la noche abierta,
cuánto rumor perdido en su esplendor.
Tal vez, alguna vez, como este oleaje,
volverán las oscuras golondrinas,
picotearán aquí y allá,
invadirán tejados y glorietas;
volverán sin sus nombres.
Pero allí estará el mar, preciso y leve,
sin disfraces ni máscaras,
sin otra ceremonia
que nosotros aquí, cuerpo a cuerpo,
ciudad incluida, ardiendo.

AN INVITATION TO GO BEYOND THE MATERIAL

It is difficult not to find solemnity and enchantment
in this night by the sea, city and all.
The show never ends:
yesterday's waves, flotsam from days before,
grounded ghosts, dimly lit windows
and avenues and bodies.
History reigns here, its mysteries, its ironies;
the music of yesteryear does not regret the past
and your body and my body slide along
as if searching for mirrors, as forests aflame,
before this immenseness that sings silently,
before this chatty little nothing
of avenues, cats and pitiful places.
Look at this sea: words aren't for naught;
such serene wisdom in its rhythms,
such constancy to counter the vastness of night,
such murmuring lost in its grandeur.
Maybe, someday, as with the coming waves,
the dark swallows will return,
they will peck here and there,
they will invade houses and arbors;
they will return stealthily.
But there will be the sea,
imposing and gentle,
no costumes, no masks,
no other spectacle
just the two of us here, body against body,
city and all, burning.

MÍA GALLEGOS

EL CLAUSTRO ELEGIDO

No busco nada.
A nadie aguardo en este día.

Esperar es una de las raras
estratagemas de Dios
para detenernos en un punto.

Mi país:
montaña verde y lluvia.
Un caballo se pierde en la llanura
imaginada,
que ahora está vedada a mis ojos.

Busco la intensa reflexión:
la de los libros amigos,
la luz interna que preciso para vivir,
el candil de oro,
el Eclesiastés y la paciencia de Job.

A mi edad y en un país de lluvia,
el claustro es una elección.

Ahí se pierden los contornos.
La vida se diluye en un ir y venir
del trabajo al café,
del café a la taberna.

MÍA GALLEGOS

ALONE BY CHOICE

I'm not looking for anything.
Not expecting anyone today.

Expectation is one of God's little tricks
that keeps us frozen
in one spot.

My homeland:
green mountains and rainfall.
A horse is lost
on the imaginary plain,
now shielded from my eyes.

I am looking for intense reflection:
like in my favorite books,
the interior light that I need in order to live,
the gold candle,
Ecclesiastes and the patience of Job.

At my age and in a country of rain,
solitude is a choice.

Forms lose their shape there.
Life is a matter of coming and going
from work to the café,
from the café to the bar.

Busco la infancia que soy:
la llanura, la sombra del árbol gigantesco,
el único mar sin fondo,
el caballo desbocado en su furia,
el verdor de la montaña junto al cielo.

Me gusta quedarme a solas
sintiendo cómo la sangre me nutre de nuevas vestiduras.

A solas me pertenezco.
No hay dicotomía entre el espejo y yo.
Una vive y la otra sueña.
Juntas recordamos a un hombre.
Juntas hemos escrito estos versos.

I am looking for the child that I am:
the plain, the shade of that gigantic tree,
the endless, bottomless sea,
the runaway horse in all its fury,
the green of the mountain against the sky.

I like to be alone
feeling my blood making me new.

When I'm alone I belong to myself.
There's no separation between me and the mirror.
One lives and the other dreams.
Together we remember a man.
Together we wrote these verses.

LOS DONES

La sinceridad interior no es una virtud,
la ternura no es un don.
La capacidad de amor asusta,
la valentía es un arma de doble filo.

Nada me fue dado gratuitamente.

El acicate más fuerte es la autenticidad,
la vida en sí misma vale por su intensidad.

La soledad sin fantasía es dura.
La soledad sublimada también es dura.
Vencer es culminar con la batalla íntima.
No existe un don sin su contrario.
Nada existe en estado puro.

Vivo con la paradoja de la sensibilidad.
Acepto la soledad total,
como la llama viva,
la lucidez con los fantasmas
y a veces, descanso la cabeza sobre ti, abuelo,
y nada más.

Sé que la pluma se maneja con la misma fuerza
                                    [que la espada.
Yo también con los años he aprendido algo de esgrima.

GIFTS

Sincerity is not a virtue when you keep it to yourself;
tenderness is not a gift.
The capacity to love is frightening,
courage is a double-edged sword.

Nothing was ever given to me for free.

Authenticity is the strongest motivator;
life is worth the trouble because it's so intense.

Loneliness without a dream is hard.
Sublimated loneliness is also hard.
To triumph is to put an end to the interior struggle.
There is no gift without a counterpart.
Nothing exists in a pure state.

I live within the paradox of sensitivity.
I accept complete loneliness,
like a burning flame.
My ghosts are clear to me.
And sometimes I rest my head on your shoulder,
                                              [grandfather,
and nothing more.

I know that the pen is as powerful as the sword.
Over the years, I too have learned something about fencing.

TIEMPO DE DANZAR

No. Yo no me ato al tiempo perecedero.
Busco más bien
el otro tiempo, el del ropaje íntimo.

En la historia entre tú y yo,
elegí ser Cresida y sonrío.
Descreo de las guerras y de los tiranos.
Y por ello me recordarás.

Soy griega y siempre lo seré.
Cuando cesa mi llanto empieza mi danza.
Y danzo porque conozco el placer.
Recupero el tiempo de los dioses.

He nacido, he vuelto a nacer y sonrío,
porque mío es el amor. Yo soy el amor.
A mí me venció el amor.

Ha nacido en mí la mujer
que encuentra la misma dulzura
en el amor que triunfa
y en el amor que fracasa.
Retorno a mi tiempo de las moradas infinitas,
al que pertenezco.

Es el tiempo de mi danza.
Yo soy griega
y por ello me recordarás.

TIME TO DANCE

No. I'm not tied to mortal time.
I am searching for the other time,
the one hidden behind flowing robes.

In our story, yours and mine,
I decided to be Cressida*, and I smile.
I don't believe in wars or tyrants.
And you will remember me for that.

I am Greek and always will be.
When I stop crying, I start dancing.
And I dance because I know what pleasure is about.
I am reliving the time of the gods.

I was born, and born again, and I smile
because love is mine. I am love.
Love has conquered me.

The woman in me finds
the love that triumphs
just as sweet
as the love that fails.
I go back to my time of countless abodes,
the time where I belong.

It is the time of my dance.
I am Greek
and you will remember me for that.

Es mío el amor. Yo soy el amor.
Este es mi tiempo de las horas
profundas.

Sonrío y te dejo pasar.

Love is mine. I am love.
This is my time
when the hours become intense.

I smile and let you go by.

ADRIANO CORRALES

PINOS Y ARAUCARIAS

Pinos y araucarias comadrean con las palmeras

Una garza se aferra ante las luces que caen

Las copas espumean su ademán salvaje

Las frases atraviesan las gargantas
como dioses desconocidos
en esta tierra cavada árbol arriba
con ríos de estiércol y lunas frías

El paisaje se nos muere
soles blancos
      sobre soles negros
descargan el agua que se encharca
como el tiempo en nuestros días

ADRIANO CORRALES

THE PINES AND THE ARAUCARIAS

The pines and the araucarias gossip with the palms

A heron holds on as the light falls

Glasses gesture wildly with overflowing foam

Sentences come out of throats
like unrecognized gods
in this land of uprooted trees
with rivers of manure and cold moons

The scenery is dying before our eyes
white suns
              over black suns
strip away the water that pools together
like the time in our days

LA PIEDRA SE FROTA CONTRA OTRA PIEDRA

La piedra se frota contra otra piedra
para cincelar el fuego en luces que configuran
la paloma torcaz sangrada por manos fundadoras

Así froto estas palabras en el centro del túmulo
para restituir la luz en la imagen calcinada
como el primer planeta verde en la hoguera

Así chispeantes y amorosas
por la noche dividida de los cuerpos
en dos fauces para coser el silencio
sin alas en la ringlera de satélites y astros
desangrándose como mi perfil sobre la mesa

THE STONE STRIKES ANOTHER STONE

The stone strikes another stone
starting a fire whose light outlines
the wood dove bled out by powerful hands

So do I strike these words in the center of the tomb
to restore the light in the charred image
as did the first green planet in the conflagration

So they fly sparkling and loving
through the shared darkness
two bodies a gaping maw to stitch out the silence
wingless through the rings of planets and orbs
bleeding away like my silhouette on the table

EN EL FONDO DE LA TARDE

En el fondo de la tarde
con la arboleda frutal de cámara verde
recuerdo a Madre pedaleando
sobre esa magnífica estructura
de metales fundidos y madreas preciosas
en cuyo centro de hierro forjado
podíamos deletrear S-I-N-G-E-R
igual a Robert Crawford el poeta escocés

La aguja trazaba veredas de pájaros
estelas de pececillos escarlatas
cantos de ojales decorados
y cuando se salía de su ruta
Ella sin lentes detenía mi lectura
para que le ayudase a pasar el hilo de tiempo
por el orificio de la nada

Hoy que barajo lentamente esas imágenes
mientras mi esposa en el taller
pinta figuras obesas de barro y canto
percibo el ronroneo del pedal bajo el escritorio
y las manos de Madre enhebran las palabras
sobre camisas y blusas de otra tarde
en que versos y esculturas son canciones
de una máquina en el viento

LATE IN THE AFTERNOON

Late in the afternoon
along with the green circus tent of the fruit orchard
I remember Mother pedaling
on that magnificent machine
of fashioned metal and precious wood
where we could spell out
on its cast iron center S-I-N-G-E-R
like the Scottish poet Robert Crawford*

The needle outlined bird trails
wakes behind little scarlet fishes
decorated edges of buttonholes
and when she would take a break
taking her glasses off she would interrupt my reading
to help her pass the thread of time
through the needle of nothingness

Today I slowly ponder these images
while in her studio my wife
paints her squatty figures of clay and stone
I hear the hum of the pedal beneath the desk
and my mother's hands stitch words
on the shirts and blouses of another afternoon
where verses and sculptures are the songs
of a machine in the wind

© Carlos Kidd

ANA ISTARÚ

DE DÓNDE HAS LLEGADO

De dónde has llegado,
hombre dormido.
Qué nube te vertió,
qué carabela.
Quién te autoriza a este derrame
de nenúfares,
quién deslizó en tu tez
el pájaro de plata.
Te posas en mi lecho con descuido:
eres un ángel olvidado
dentro de un camarote.
Yo no comprendo este hombre
tan extenso.
No puedo ya dormir: mi sábana
se empeña en ser un viento alisio,
la flor de la lavanda.
Mi almohada, que retoma
su viaje de gaviotas.
Mis antiguos zapatos, dos erizos.
y este hombre pequeñito,
desnudo sin siquiera una gardenia.
Por qué mi mano vuela
a su incauta porcelana,
a su carne de membrillos.
Qué contratiempo.

ANA ISTARÚ

WHERE DID YOU COME FROM

Where did you come from,
sleeping man.
What cloud dropped you,
what caravel.
Who allowed you to pour out
these water lilies,
who slipped that shiny plumage
into your skin.
You carelessly alight on my bed:
a forgotten angel
imprisoned in my cabin.
I do not understand
the vastness of this man.
I can no longer sleep: my sheets
insist on being hot southern wind,
lavender flowers.
My pillow wants to fly
like a gull on the wing.
My shoes have become thorny little creatures.
And here's this naked little man
without even a fig leaf.
Why does my hand fly
to his unsuspecting whiteness,
to his sweet inviting flesh.
What a problem.

Qué miraré otra vez ya nunca
si sólo puedo mirar mi visitante.
De dónde vino la zarza de tu ceja,
los dos puntos de cobre de tu tórax.
Qué pana buscaré,
si no tu vello.
Qué vaso, qué beso,
qué ribera sin tu boca,
hombre dormido.
Qué pan de oro
sin tu sueño.

What will I ever look at again
if all I can look at is my visitor.
Where did that bush of eyebrows come from,
those two copper coins on your chest.
What cover will I seek,
if not the hair on your chest.
What glass, what kiss,
what landing without your lips,
sleeping man.
What loaf of gold
without your presence.

AHORA QUE EL AMOR

Ahora que el amor
es una extraña costumbre,
extinta especie
de la que hablan
documentos antiguos,
y se censura el oficio desusado
de la entrega;
ahora que el vientre
olvidó engendrar hijos,
y el tobillo su gracia
y el pezón su promesa feliz
de miel y esencia;
ahora que la carne se anuda
y se desnuda,
anda y revolotea
sobre la carne buena
sin dejar perfumes, semilla,
batallas victoriosas,
y recogiendo en cambio
redondas cosechas;
ahora que es velada la ternura,
modalidad perdida de las abuelas,
que extravió la caricia
su avena generosa;
ahora que la piel
de las paredes se palpan
varón y mujer
sin alcanzar el mirto,

NOW THAT LOVE

Now that love
is a curious custom,
an extinct species
only mentioned
in ancient tomes,
and the antiquated practice of surrender
is criticized;
now that the womb
no longer bears children,
and the ankle has lost its grace
as the nipple has lost its sweet promise
of honey and life;
now that flesh entwines
and unwinds
rolls and rides
over good flesh
without leaving a scent, a seed,
or a sense of the battle won,
gathering in, on the other hand,
bountiful harvests;
now that tenderness is forbidden,
a forgotten practice from grandma's day,
and the caress has lost
its generous sustenance;
now that the walls themselves
male and female
stroke each other
but reach not the rose,

la brasa estremecida,
ardo sencillamente,
encinta y embriagada.
Rescato la palabra primera
del útero,
y clásica y extravagante
emprendo la tarea
de despojarme.
Y amo.

the embers being shaken,
I burn anew,
pregnant and intoxicated.
I ransom the primal
word of the womb
and timeless,
though out of place,
I set about the task
of undressing.
And I love.

ÁBRETE SEXO

Ábrete sexo
como una flor que accede,
descorre las aldabas de tu ermita,
deja escapar
al nadador transido,
desiste, no retengas
sus frágiles cabriolas,
ábrete con arrojo,
como un halcón que emerge
y ostenta sobre el aire sus geranios.
Desenfunda,
oh poza de penumbra, tu misterio.
No detengas su viaje al navegante.
No importa que su adiós
te hiera como cierzo,
como rayo de hielo que en la pelvis
aloja sus astillas.
Ábrete sexo,
hazte cascada,
olvida tu tristeza.
Deja partir al niño
que vive en tu entresueño.
Abre gallardamente
tus cálidas compuertas
a este copo de mieles,
a este animal que tiembla
como un jirón de viento,
a este fruto rugoso

OPEN UP LITTLE GIRL

Open up little girl
like a flower giving in,
slide back the bolt on the chapel door,
let that overwhelmed little swimmer
escape,
let go, do not interrupt
his delicate pirouettes,
open with flourish
like a protruding balcony
showing off its geraniums for all to see.
Reveal your mysteries,
oh tunnel of twilight.
Do not hamper the traveler along his way.
Little matter if his farewell
wounds like a north wind
like a bolt of ice planting splinters
in your pelvis.
Open up little girl,
become a cascade,
forget your sadness.
Let the child
living in the shadows
go free.
Open your hot flood gates gallantly
to this bundle of sweetness,
to this animal that trembles
like a gust of wind,
to this wrinkled fruit

que va a hundirse en la luz con arrebato,
a buscar como un ciervo con los ojos cerrados
los pezones del aire, los dos senos del día.

about to explode into the light,
to suckle like a fawn with its eyes closed
the nipples of fresh air, the breasts of daylight.

© Carlos Kidd

CARLOS CORTÉS

PEREGRINACIÓN DEL AGUAFIESTAS

En el último milenio hemos oído un gentil aleteo
para mudos
mientras amanece en el centro del centro de américa
el pájaro de fuego bate sus alas de espuma
en el bravío torrente de primavera
amanece el mundo en un árbol espléndido
sus raíces destruyen el tiempo
de las necrópolis imperiales
pero mi alma lleva la señal de la boca tapada
apenas balbuceo estas concherías
de fin de siglo
        jeroglíficos de neón
en un país condenado a la asfixia
¿cuál es el color del cielo
visto a través de un claro entre las nubes
en mitad de la lluvia?
como un modesto mercachifle busco en el diccionario
el secreto de las palabras

CARLOS CORTÉS

PILGRIMAGE OF A WET BLANKET

In the last millennium we have been hearing
a gentle fluttering for mutes
while awakening in the center of the center of America
the fire bird beats its frothy wings
in the ferocious torrent of spring
the world awakens in a magnificent tree
whose roots are destroying the age
of the imperial necropolis
but my soul bears the stigma of being tight lipped
I am barely able to babble these quaint rhymes
from the end of the century
                         neon hieroglyphics
in a land condemned to asphyxia
what color is the sky
when seen through a break in the clouds
in the middle of a storm?
like a poor street vendor I search the dictionary
for the secret meaning of words

ALEGORÍA DEL QUETZAL

Con la cabeza encendida
y la boca llameante
en la selva del viento
mientras amanece y anochece
    tanto a la vez
en los surcos donde la tierra
como un nuevo cielo
se vuelve transparente y alada
espejea un colibrí de fuego
una ocarina raya la tela azul del cielo
como una pedrada en el follaje líquido
de la laguna que provoca anillos en el agua
       el quetzal
—jade emplumado de escalofriantes ramas—
vuelca su esquiva nitidez sobre los hombres
y llueve y todo es alero y lluvia
y así   unidos y vivos
     sin piel   sin muertos
sin guerras ni paces misterios o monumentos
mansamente mediocres
risiblemente pequeños como el quetzal que muere
en su cautiverio
discretamente ingenuos y asombrados del asombro propio
¿a quién pedirle permiso para ver?
¿a quién agradecerle por tanto y por tan poco?

ALLEGORY OF THE QUEZTAL

His head on fire
mouth flaming
in the wind-blown forest
while day breaks and night falls
    at the same time
in the furrows where the earth
like a new sky
becomes transparent and swift
a fiery hummingbird shimmers
while ancient music scratches the blue fabric of the sky
like a stone thrown into the liquid foliage
of the lagoon making rings in the water
       the quetzal
—jade fletched with terrifying branches—
pours his timid clarity over mankind
and it rains and everything is shelter and rain
and so   together and alive
    without skin   without fatalities
with neither war nor peace, mysteries or monuments,
mildly mediocre,
derisively small, like the quetzal that dies
in his cage,
discreetly naïve and astonished by our own astonishment.
whom do we ask for permission to see?
whom do we thank for so much and so little?

BOLERO SIN TIEMPO

*A la memoria de Dante Polimeni**

Un hombre/mujer/género o especie
uno solo
unigénito único huérfano de sí mismo
uno solo
entrañable en su celeste desnudez
iluminado por la flaqueza
innumerable en su cuerpo malherido
un hombre/mujer/género o especie
miserable nominal vivo
un átomo de melancolía en el cosmos increado y ajeno
un hombre tan solo tan poco casi nada
hediondo por su tristeza
resplandeciente en su sola soledad
un hombre/mujer/género o especie
uno solo
minoría entre la muchedumbre animal y vegetal
uno solo
paria bastardo apestado intocable
uno solo
tan poca cosa
casi/casi nada
es suficiente para mí
uno solo
una nada en el mar de la nada
un don nadie en el torbellino de ninguna parte
uno solo

THE TIMELESS BOLERO

In memory of Dante Polimeni*

One man/woman/genus or species
just one
one single orphan only-begotten to him/herself
irresistible in his heavenly nakedness
irradiated by her skinniness
innumerable in his/her badly wounded body
one man/woman/genus or species
one miserable living nothing
an atom of melancholy in a yet to be created and alien
                                                      [cosmos
a man so alone so small nearly nothing
stinking in his sadness
radiant in his lonely loneliness
one man/woman/genus or species
just one
a minority between the animal and vegetable world
just one
bastard pariah infected untouchable
just one
such a little thing
nearly almost nothing
is enough for me
just one
a nothing in a sea of nothingness
a mister nobody in a whirlwind from nowhere
just one

---

es suficiente para amar
para inventar el amor
para cantar el amor
para inventar todas las palabras con qué decir una vez más
y para siempre
amor te amo vos sos mi amor

is enough to love
to invent love
to sing of love
to invent every word used to say once more
and for always
love I love you you are my love

© Carlos Kidd

LUIS CHAVES

MI HERMANO CREE QUE EL PRIMER NOMBRE
DE DICKINSON ES ANGIE

Con el gato dentro del saco de gangoche
montamos los dos la misma bicicleta.
Luego nuestras cabezas fuera de la baranda
vieron cómo se hundía en el río Virilla
para morir, no ahogado,
sino por envenenamiento.

Hoy, a sus veinticuatro años
y aunque no lee lo que escribo,
mi hermano me ayuda a vender libros.
Asiste a todas mis lecturas,
lo que quiere decir, máximo,
dos noches al año;
y como no sabe quién es ese tal Eliot,
ni Vallejo, ni Dickinson,
pero le gusta conversar
cuando está con mis amigos,
les cuenta de cuando por accidente
le abrí la frente con un bate de béisbol.

La verdad no nos vemos seguido
y casi nunca directo a los ojos.
Me deja hacerle
las mismas preguntas de uso
imprimiéndole, piadosamente,
espontaneidad a sus respuestas.

LUIS CHAVES

MY BROTHER THINKS THAT
DICKINSON'S FIRST NAME IS ANGIE

With the cat in the burlap sack
we are both riding the same bike.
Next our heads are poking through the railing
to see how if you fell into the Virilla River
you would die, not of drowning,
but of poisoning.

Today he is twenty-four years old
and, even though he doesn't read what I write,
my brother helps me sell books.
He attends all of my readings,
which means, at most,
two nights a year;
and since he doesn't know who this Eliot might be,
or Vallejo, or Dickinson,
but he still likes to talk
when he's with my friends,
he tells them about the time I accidently
busted his head open with a baseball bat.

The fact is we don't see each other often
and practically never look each other in the eye.
He lets me ask him
the usual routine questions
while he, out of kindness,
tries to make his answers sound spontaneous.

Hace unos meses en un recital afirmé
con mal disimulado esnobismo,
que suelo imaginar animales.
Mi hermano, quizá el único que escuchaba
desde la última mesa, lejos de las luces,
parecía decir con su mirada de desconcierto
que él me prefería cuando los sacrificábamos.

At a reading a few months ago I stated,
with a poorly disguised tone of snobbism,
that I often imagine animals.
My brother, who may have been the only person listening
at that poorly lit table in the back,
seemed to be saying with a troubled look
that he liked me best when we were killing them.

¿TAN RÁPIDO LLEGÓ EL 2002?

El sonido de los refrigeradores
arrulla a las familias
y creen que es la lluvia
o viceversa.
Para los turistas,
esto que es tu casa
será un video amateur
de palomas que llegan a comer
de sus manos.

No hace mucho tiempo
dormíamos sin soñar
mientras nuestros pies se tocaban.
Sin duda, los primitivos
encontrarían aquí un significado.

Del cine salen los electores
a vivir una película
en que todos son extras
y nada hay en eso de dramático,
como tampoco nada excepcional
en el charco de diesel tornasolado
donde los niños escupen para divertirse.

Allí donde fue su casa
ya no está la foto en blanco y negro
de la hija de un alcohólico.

CAN IT BE 2002 ALREADY?

The hum of refrigerators
lulls families to sleep
and they think it is the rain
or vice-versa.
For the tourists,
that place that's your house
will become an amateur video
of pigeons coming to eat
from their hands.

Not long ago
we would sleep a dreamless sleep
with our feet touching.
No doubt primitive people
would find some meaning there.

The electorate leaves the movie theater
to live in a movie
where they are all extras
and there's nothing dramatic about that
just like there is nothing exceptional
about the multi-colored puddle of diesel fuel
that little boys are spitting in for fun.

There where your house used to be
there's no longer the black and white photo
of the daughter of an alcoholic.

El árbol creció con los hermanos
tiene dos iniciales encerradas
en un poliedro
que debió ser corazón.

Llamarnos por nuestros nombres
debería parecernos un milagro
o al menos algo digno
de esas películas para intelectuales.

Herencia de mi madre es hablar poco,
el resto no es culpa de nadie.
Vivo en la que fue su casa
como un turista
y es mi padre ese señor
que alimenta a las palomas.

Nos arrulló varios inviernos la lluvia
o eso queremos creer,
pero es cierto
que dormíamos sin soñar
y que nuestros pies se tocaban.

The tree that grew up with the boys
has two initials enclosed
in a form
that was supposed to be a heart.

That we call each other by name
should seem like a miracle
or at least something worthy
of those films for intellectuals.

Not talking much is something that I inherited
                              [from my mother,
the rest of me is nobody's fault.
I live in the house that was hers
like a tourist
and my father is that guy
feeding the pigeons.

The rain lulled us to sleep for several winters
or that's what we want to believe,
but the fact is
that we slept a dreamless sleep
with our feet touching.

MANCHAS DE KÉTCHUP EN LAS PÁGINAS DEL ECLESIASTÉS

—Es el bar donde ahora hay un parqueo,
  al fondo Molina escribe su bestiario,
  el dólar a doscientos, un gramo a mil.

—El primo segundo que leyó Kant
  por tres semestres
  y de noche se soñaba náufrago
  en la Isla de Gilligan.

—De la baldosa 3 a la 15
  se mueve la línea de sombra
  antes de tomar una decisión.

—Desde la barandilla del ferry:
  dos botellas no retornables
  alejándose en el golfo,
  una junto a la otra,
  la mía y la de alguno de primera clase.

—Todo lo anterior
  o tal vez la capital ya tarde en la noche
  cuando los que todavía no se fueron a dormir
  dicen *hoy* aunque técnicamente
  ya es *mañana*.

Cómo adivinar en su momento
que todo es parte de la misma sensación.
Cómo predecir
que la sensación no será pasajera.

KETCHUP STAINS ON THE PAGES
OF ECCLESIASTES

—It's the bar that has a parking lot now,
  Molina is writing his bestiary in the back.
  The dollar is at two hundred, a gram costs a thousand.

—The second cousin that studied Kant
  for three semesters
  and by night dreamed that he was shipwrecked
  on Gilligan's Island.

—The shadow on the floor
  moves from the 3rd tile to the 15th tile
  before a decision is made.

—Seen from the ferry's handrail:
  two non-returnable bottles
  drifting off into the gulf,
  one next to the other,
  mine and one from somebody in first class.

—All of the above
  or maybe the capital well into the night
  when those who haven't yet gone to sleep
  are still saying *today* even though technically
  it's already *tomorrow*.

How are we to know at the time
that everything is part of one continuum?
How do we know at the time
that the continuum will have no end?

© Carlos Kidd

NOTES

Page 19: The *yigüirro* (*Turdus grayi*), Costa Rica's national bird, slightly larger than a North American robin, and paler in color. Costa Rica could have chosen one of many other more exotic looking birds as the nation's standard bearer, but chose the *yigüirro* because of its ubiquitous nature and its tendency to live near human dwellings.

Page 53: Nazim Himket (1902-1963), Turkish poet and playwright, often considered in the West as the most outstanding Turkish writer of the twentieth century.

Page 71: Jorge Debravo, Costa Rican poet (1938-1967).

Page 77: Guillermo Sáenz-Patterson, Costa Rican poet (b. 1944).

Page 99: Cressida, a character appearing in many Medieval and Renaissance retellings of the story of the Trojan War; she is depicted as a paragon of female inconstancy.

Page 109: Robert Crawford (b. 1959), Scottish poet, scholar and critic.

Page 131: Dante Polimeni, a bookseller and friend of the poet.

About the Authors and Selected Poems

Isaac Felipe Azofeifa (1909-1997). Poet, essayist, literature professor. Author of *Trunca unidad* (1958), *Vigilia en pie de muerte* (1961), *Canción* (1964), *Estaciones* (1967), *Días y territorios* (1969), *Cima del gozo* (1974), *Cruce de vía* (1983) and *Órbita* (1997). Two of his essays are *Prosa con ton y son* (1993) and *Oficio de poesía* (2007). Selected poems: "Alegría," "El yigüirro de la madrugada," and "El sueño infinito," taken from *Órbita* (San José, Farben/Norma, 1998). © Successors of Isaac Felipe Azofeifa.

Jorge Charpentier (1933-2003). Poet and literature professor. Author of *Diferente al abismo* (1955), *Poemas para dormir a un niño blanco que dijo que no* (1959), *Rítmico salitre* (1968), *Poemas de la respuesta* (1977), *Donde duerme la mariposa* (1981), *Tú tan llena de mar* (1984), *Arrodillar la noche* (1988), *Cómplice del alba* (1991), *No preguntes la noche* (1995), and *El aroma de la rosa no consiste en la rosa* (2000). Selected poems: "Amante con amor condena," taken from *Cómplice del alba* (San José, Mesén Editores, 1991), "Entre madrugar y entrar la noche," and "Con el bastón y las manos," taken from *El aroma de la rosa no consiste en la rosa* (Heredia, Editorial Universidad Nacional, 2000). © Successors of Jorge Charpentier.

Carlos Rafael Duverrán (1935-1995). Poet, literary critic, translator and literature professor. Author of *Paraíso en la tierra* (1953), *Lujosa lejanía* (1958), *Ángel salvaje* (1959), *Poemas del corazón hecho verano* (1963), *Vendaval de tu nombre* (1967), *Estación de sueños* (1970), *Redención del día* (1971), *Tiempo grabado* (1981), and *Piedra de origen* (1998). As a translator, he published *El canto me conduce* (1998). Selected poems: "Este es mi laberinto," "Retrato de niña," and "En medio de las cosas," taken from *Piedra de origen* (Heredia, Editorial Oro y Barro, 1998). © Successors of Carlos Rafael Duverrán.

Mayra Jiménez (1939). Poet, cultural promoter and literature professor. Author of *Los trabajos del sol* (1966), *Tierra adentro* (1967), *El libro de Volumnia* (1969), *Me queda la palabra* (1993), and *Qué buena tu memoria* (2003). Editor of *Poesía de la nueva Nicaragua* (1983).

Selected poems: "Carta," "Reencuentro," and "En el río Tamarindo," taken from *Qué buena tu memoria* (San José, Editorial Costa Rica, 2001). © Mayra Jiménez.

Julieta DOBLES (1943). Poet and literature professor. Author of *Reloj de siempre* (1965), *El peso vivo* (1968), *Los pasos terrestres* (1976), *Hora de lejanías* (1982), *Los delitos de Pandora* (1987), *Una viajera demasiado azul* (1990), *Casas de la memoria* (2003), *Costa Rica poema a poema* (1997), *Hojas furtivas* (2007), *Amar en Jerusalén* (1992), *Costa Rica poema a poema* (1997), *Poemas para arrepentidos* (2003), *Casas de la memoria* (2003), and *Hojas furtivas* (2007). Selected poems: "Casa en el sueño," taken from *Casas de la memoria* (San José, Editorial Universidad de Costa Rica, 2003), "Descubrimiento," and "La casa enamorada," taken from *Hojas furtivas* (San José, Editorial Costa Rica, 2007). © Julieta Dobles.

Rodrigo QUIRÓS (1944-1997). Poet, translator, instructor of English language and literature. Author of *Después de nacer* (1967), *Abismo sitiado* (1973), *En defensa del tiempo* (1977), *Del sueño a la jornada* (1979), *A tientas en la luz* (1982), and *Alturas de la sangre* (1998). Selcted poems: "Conversaciones con Debravo," "El malinformado," and "Este sol, mi Señor," taken from *Alturas de la sangre* (San José, Editorial de la Universidad Estatal a Distancia, 1998). © Successors of Rodrigo Quirós.

Carlos Francisco MONGE (1951). Poet, essayist and literature professor. Author of *Astro y labio* (1972), *A los pies de la tiniebla* (1972), *Población del asombro* (1975), *Reino del latido* (1978), *Los fértiles horarios* (1983), *La tinta extinta* (1990), *Enigmas de la imperfección* (2002), *Fábula umbría* (2009) and *Poemas para una ciudad inerme* (2009). His essays include *La imagen separada* (1984), *La rama de fresno* (1999), *El vanguardismo literario en Costa Rica* (2005), and *Territorios y figuraciones* (2009). Selected poems: "Profanación del Quijote," taken from *Enigmas de la imperfección* (Heredia, Editorial Universidad Nacional, 2002), "Poema del encino," taken from *Fábula umbría* (San José, Editorial Costa Rica, 2009), and "Invitación a disolver la materia," taken from *Poemas para una ciudad inerme* (San José, Editorial de la Universidad Estatal a Distancia, 2009). © Carlos Francisco Monge.

Mía GALLEGOS (1953). Poet, instructor of Spanish language and literature, journalist of cultural affairs. Author of *Golpe de albas* (1977), *Los reductos del sol* (1985), *El claustro elegido* (1989), and *Los días y los sueños* (1995). Selected poems: "El claustro elegido," "Los dones," and "Tiempo de danzar," taken from *El claustro elegido* (San José, Editorial de la Universidad Estatal a Distancia, 1989). © Mía Gallegos.

Adriano CORRALES (1958). Poet, novelist and essayist. Author of *Tranvía negro* (1995), *La suerte del andariego* (1999), *Hacha encendida* (2000), *Profesión u oficio* (2002), *Caza de poeta* (2004), and *Kabanga* (2008). His novels and short stories include *Los ojos del antifaz* (1999), *El jabalí de la media luna* (2003) and *Balalaika en clave de son* (2005). He is the editor of *Antología de la poesía costarricense contemporánea* (2007). Selected poems: "Pinos y araucarias," taken from *Tranvía negro* (San José, Arboleda Ediciones, 2010), "La piedra se frota contra otra piedra," taken from *Hacha encendida* (San José, Arboleda Ediciones, 2008), and "En el fondo de la tarde," taken from *Caza del poeta* (San José, Ediciones Andrómeda, 2004). © Adriano Corrales.

Ana ISTARÚ (1960). Poet, playwright and actress. Author of *Palabra nueva* (1975), *Poemas para un día cualquiera* (1977), *Poemas abiertos y otros amaneceres* (1980), *La estación de fiebre* (1983), *La muerte y otros efímeros agravios* (1989), and *Verbo madre* (1995). Her plays include *El vuelo de la grulla* (1984), *Madre nuestra que estás en la tierra* (1998), *Hombres en escabeche* (2000), *Baby boom en el Paraíso* (1995), and *Sexus benedictus* (2003). Selected poems: "De dónde has llegado," "Ahora que el amor," taken from *Estación de fiebre* (San José, Editorial Universitaria Centroamericana, 1983), and "Ábrete sexo," taken from *Verbo madre* (San José, Editorial Mujeres, 1995). © Ana Istarú.

Carlos CORTÉS (1961). Poet, novelist, essayist and journalist. Author of *Erratas advertidas* (1985*)*, *Los pasos cantados* (1987), *¡El amor es esa bestia platónica!* (1991), *Cantos sumergidos* (1993), *Canciones del prodigioso citarista* (1998), and *Autorretrato y cruci/ficciones* (2006). As a novelist, he published *Cruz de olvido* (1999), and *Tanda de cuatro* *con Laura* (2002). Editor of *Poésie costaricienne du xxᵉ siècle*. Selected poems: "Peregrinación del aguafiestas," "Alegoría del quetzal," and "Bolero sin tiempo," taken from *Canciones del prodigioso citarista* (León, Diputación de León, 1998). © Carlos Cortés.

Luis CHAVES (1969). Poet and translator. Author of *El anónimo* (1996), *Los animales que imaginamos* (1998), *Historias Polaroid* (2000), *Chan Marshall* (2005), and *La máquina de hacer niebla* (2012). Editor of *Antología de la nueva poesía costarricense* (2001). Selected poems: "Mi hermano cree que el primer nombre de Dickinson es Angie," taken from *Historias Polaroid* (San José, Ediciones Perro Azul, 2000), "¿Tan rápido llegó el 2002?," and "Manchas de kétchup en las páginas del Eclesiastés," taken from *Chan Marshall* (Madrid, Visor Libros, 2005). © Luis Chaves.

ABOUT THE TRANSLATOR

Victor S. Drescher has a Master's degree in the teaching of French as a foreign language from the Sorbonne, University of Paris, and a Doctorate of Modern Languages (DML) from Middlebury College in Vermont. In 2007, he retired from Indiana University of Pennsylvania (IUP) where he taught French and Spanish and served as Director of the Critical Languages Program, and Director of Foreign Language Study and Internship Abroad Programs. In his 35 years of service to IUP, he created study abroad programs and exchange programs with universities in France, Germany, Mexico, and Costa Rica. In 1992, he founded a center for translation, IUP Translation Services. His publications include articles in the *Modern Language Journal* and a bilingual volume of poetry by Carlos Francisco Monge entitled *La tinta extinta/Invisible Ink*.

www.ingramcontent.com/pod-product-compliance
Lightning Source LLC
Chambersburg PA
CBHW020500030426
42337CB00011B/180